AQUEDUCT

AQUEDUCT

Poems

Joel Thomas Katz

DUTCH POET PRESS

2023

Copyright © 2023
Joel Thomas Katz
and Dutch Poet Press
All Rights Reserved.

ISBN: 978-1-7342742-5-7

DUTCH POET PRESS
Palo Alto, Califonia
dutchpoetpress.com

Picture Credit: The front cover image of the aqueduct of Pont du Gard constructed in Lego blocks was created by Greg S., a student of industrial engineering from Belgium who participated in the Lego Ideas program that can be found at ideas.lego.com.

CONTENTS

3 Picture Postcard: Man reclining on...

5 Dream Log

6 Snapple Fact #1368: "A neutron star is as dense as stuffing fifty million elephants into a thimble."

7 Blacksmith

8 Right Now

9 The dream was...

10 Boeing 737, Window Seat

11 Last night's dream...

12 "Every canoe is a sad canoe..." (Dean Young)

13 The dream was...

15 Interlude: Short Essay on Sleep

17 Worlds

18 Kine

19 Diptych

20 Whelk

21 The dream was...

22 "I was thinking about the potato salad in an unstable environment..." (James Tate)

23 The forest was tired...

24 Angel Coma

27 Picture Postcard: Woman climbing into...

28 NOTES

29 ACKNOWLEDGMENTS

30 COLOPHON

For Penny:
fellow dreamer

"Yesterday, you constructed an aqueduct of dreams"

Arthur Sze

Picture Postcard: Man reclining on ...

A man

a man lying

a man lying on piles of flattened car bodies

on his back with eyes closed
dressed in white shirt and black pants

he dreams of Italy

he dreams of pasta

he dreams of lasagna
because there are six layers of crushed cars beneath him
Fiats
Alfa Romeos
Lamborghinis

Any place is a place for dreaming

even hard ruins

DREAM LOG

Inside it I managed to say *This is a dream*.

I was emptying my heart of the freeway
but the dream got tired and so halted itself.

It was not the one I had planned on.

It was different than the one with atoms clanking against each other

or the one across the street from a school,
children milling around, ringed by dumpsters.

Toward the end I said *This is still a dream*.

In Hebrew "dream" is *khalóm*,
just one letter away from *khalón* "window."

Snapple Fact #1368: "A neutron star is as dense as stuffing fifty million elephants into a thimble."

I feel the need to create something light
and more roomy, a space for someone to enter.
I tell my sister that since May,
it's been five months and Dad
has yet to appear in a dream of mine. She says
Did you ask him in?

BLACKSMITH

Today you are an animal, whacking a metal arm
into an idea

what the bellows add: elbow-room

the sparks: drama

and your tongs: detachment

Today you are an animal
— some other day, just a washcloth

Heating the metal over the forge
turns it into what a dream isn't
— durable

Again and again: whack, sparks, hiss of cold water

A dream lasts till the coals die
and that is the end of one night

an ingot

RIGHT NOW

Not rain-cleared and fresh like the dream last night
(very June-y, very clock-of-fire): all those genes ladling themselves
into little beings while a crowd pressed against the window,
a cuckoo struck the hour then out slid Maureen on her mini-tractor
and Dad rose over the store.

Right now in the garage:
suitcase, suitcase, suitcase, suitcase, suitcase   no dreams

Right now: mutt still barking in the hundredth fog.

The dream was ...

The dream was a paper bag with two eyehole slits

The dream oozed off the counter onto a just-polished
    wooden floor

The dream did not work as advertised

— Did you see the dream pass by?
— No, but I caught a faint whiff of bleach ...

BOEING 737, WINDOW SEAT

People on my plane have lots to say.

The carpenter's plane has something to tell

the plank — all those dropped feathers.

Meanwhile the woods are busy

quieting hikers becoming a forest.

This morning a guy outside Starbucks

said "The next time I get knocked unconscious,

I'm gonna tell the Lord 'Don't feature me in your

stinking soul parade.' " His vow

now an airflow lifting the seventy-four

tons of my plane. The sky is stupid with clouds.

Last night the dream tried to withhold

then relented and said *Not everything is a dream...*

you've been granted words and so many ways to stumble.

Last night's dream...

involved a thick-heeled flamenco shoe
floating along a lit corridor, leading
five *bailaoras* who slowly
stamped their way along, arms proud:
no frilly dresses or castanets,
no combs in pulled-back hair —
nothing extra, just the sound ...
a message for me
or for my sister, who's reached an impasse
with her flamenco lessons:
what to do now in her Pittsburgh attic
with its wood floors and full-length mirror
for checking her footwork? Maybe
we should both dance "a clean dream ...
and make more mistakes than yesterday"

"Every canoe is a sad canoe..." (Dean Young)

every pin cushion a whoopee cushion,
every can of salted nuts an excuse
for a snake to kaboom your heart.
But why *sad*? You paddle toward the skimpy horizon
for ten hours to get only halfway
then you wake up and today's no further along
but there's a nearby Hudson's Bay store
with furs and real gold and stocking-stuffers
like pin cushions and salted nuts —
> (sad Henry Hudson
> trying to find a Northeast Passage to China...
> In 1610 his ship got trapped in ice
> then thawed but by June
> his crew had enough and set Henry adrift
> in a small boat on what is now called
> Hudson Bay)

— then you wake up: same old canoe,
same old paddle.

The dream was...

The dream was radish slices

                    slightly astringent

Interlude: Short Essay on Sleep

> *Don't be silly*
> *like a pillow full of atoms*
> —Lisa Fishman

Sleep like soup, sharing two letters and the same consistency.

Sleep gathers in the corners. Soup nests.

Soup may contain letters and sleep may contain words.

Soup doesn't intentionally misspell, and dreams don't intentionally mislead.

Through symbiosis, one may dream of soup.

Sleep is to dreams as tureen is to vegetables.

Bread goes well with sleep.

Soup rises, sleep descends.

Sleep can be punctured like a tire, though people seldom tire of soup.

Soup deprivation is not dangerous.

Soup happens when lightning hits a bowl of sleep.

WORLDS

Only in her dreams does my wife grow
a penis and the man next door

point at her and shout
What a Woodie!

+++

Only in my dreams do I have
a daughter alongside three real sons

+++

At our synagogue, a cloud of bees swarms
the rosebush where a queen has flown.

The rabbi has to call the city,
so fierce and protective the drones.

+++

The first time my love and I
saw each other naked,

I had nothing to hide behind —
finally.

KINE

Every other cow swats her tail at the daytime moon. The rest maintain a grating silence — or are they asleep standing open-eyed? In their dreams cows perceive the days lengthening. Some notice a circle of nearby humans closing and opening their mouths. The odd-numbered cows decide to lie down and smother some grass. The even's worry their multiple teats, superior to whatever humans have. The moon scoots over a bit. Half the cows are chewing over what else to do. They conclude that odd and even do not apply to humans.

DIPTYCH

Fog-Bible. For the Perplexed. In what way does fog speak to our befuddlement? It forms a pillow where one finds comfort from the insistent. Animals know they are asleep. And animals know they are dreaming (even the armadillo who rolls up into a leathery shell when attacked, even the dancing horses of Apatzingán).

You dip your hands into the waters because you are dumbstruck, then dip your hands again to find words for it. The stream is unconcerned, busy being aqueous. When everything shimmers from accumulated proximity, then what? Animals know they are dreaming when humans become silent.

WHELK

When you shared the dream in which you'd forgotten
how to use Uber, I heard it as "I'd forgotten how to use
a zipper."

Then I shared a dream where my father
first returns seven months after his funeral:
I'm in the middle of providing
a urine sample and he just walks into the exam room,
me in my sixties, him in his forties. He looks concerned.
"Is everything all right?" and I reply
"Yes, it's all routine."

A delay and then a dream — is it enough?

One day we trudged to the beach and discovered
an empty shell left behind by a whelk,
its coloration a cross between smudge and splatter.

Tell me again how we never stop dreaming because
there's no end to ~~confusion~~ comfort.

The dream was...

The dream was an EXIT sign, red in a darkened theater

      a misplaced can opener

            scarecrow in a field of no corn

"I was thinking about the potato salad in an unstable environment…" (James Tate)

— how it threatens the city's potholed streets and tenements with its picnic exuberance, how potato salad overshadows main dishes and, being unstable, sheds its isotopes, eventually leaving behind an inert radiance

— or is the *viewer* unstable and a potato salad is a potato salad is a potato salad? Does it matter whether it's served on fine china versus stuffed into a take-away carton from the local deli? In a world swirling with spatchcocked chicken and helium-chilled peach foam, I would choose the potato salad take-away carton eight times out of ten. Yet between two dreams, I'd pick the one more convoluted.

The forest was tired…

and really needed a break from
being a forest — all those animals,
all that shade! — wanted
a stand-in for a few hours
o how the forest longed
for a compact situation: cafe,
bowling alley or an art
house movie (so appealing
mid-day)
      and why not
take off the *entire* day
or even a weekend? it all came down
to the pool of availables
it was time to contact Place Holders™
see if anyone was free . . .
then the forest decided
not to return, the stand-in stranded
in the clearing, waiting waiting till
the only thing to do was call
and report a forest missing

ANGEL COMA

> *Angels visit because they're curious*
> *about our condition, not having*
> *any children of their own.*
> — P.B. Almoni

Not last week's disoriented angel
who kept bumping into fences
and wore a robe of scars.

Nor yesterday's angel who suffered
a stroke, left wing drooping,
flying in circles.

Today was different.
One particular angel fell

into a coma. How could that even
happen? A cohort of healthy angels
gathered around their stricken one,

each creature's wings touching its neighbors.
They gazed at the motionless one,
each praying to be spared.

Truth is, like humans
some angels are more ready
than others.

Picture Postcard: Woman climbing into…

A woman in high heels and black gloves holding a branch
in her left hand is trying to hoist her body into a ship's porthole,

her upper half already through the circular opening,
left arm with the branch not yet inside.

The branch, held upright, looks like a wooden candelabra.

Her legs are lifted and tucked against her bottom so the heels
stick out at odd angles.

What you don't notice at first: the rivets along the top half
of the open porthole

or in the bottom right corner of the photo: a metal cleat for
ropes, at the same angle as her still-struggling torso.

The rivets, the cleat, the metal ladder to the left of the porthole—
what else slips past you

as the woman climbs back into her dream?

NOTES

The epigraph comes from Arthur Sze's poem "First Snow" in his book *Sight Lines* (Copper Canyon Press, 2019).

The poem "Man reclining on..." (page 3) is in conversation with the following image by Swedish photographer Maria Friberg:

https://www.artnet.com/artists/maria-friberg/still-lives-5-tfMyeL1STn7k-XR4U4CBig2

"Last night's dream" (page 11): the components of Spanish flamenco include *cante* (singing), *toque* (guitar playing) and *baile* (dance). A female flamenco dancer is a *bailaora*. The quote is a rephrased version of a line from Gertrude Stein's *Tender Buttons*.

The title "Every canoe is a sad canoe... (Dean Young)" on page 12 is taken from a phrase in his poem "Bunny Tract" (*Embryoyo*, 2007).

The title "I was thinking about the potato salad in an unstable environment... (James Tate)" on page 22 is taken from a phrase in his poem "Like a Scarf" (*Worshipful Company of Fletchers*, 1994).

The poem "Woman climbing into..." on page 27 is in conversation with the following photo image:

https://www.reddit.com/r/Damnthatsinteresting/comments/zud88n/a_woman_holding_a_mistletoe_got_pulled_through_a/

ACKNOWLEDGMENTS

Grateful acknowledgment to the editors of *DMQ Review* (online), where a version of my poem "I was thinking about the potato salad in an unstable environment..." (James Tate) appears in their third Prose Poem special issue (Spring 2023), and to the editors of *Caesura* (pcsj.com/caesura), where my poem "Diptych" will appear in the Fall 2023 issue with the theme "Objects in the Mirror."

Thanks to various readers who commented on earlier versions of these poems: Kathryn Abelson, Jane Jacobson, Joy Katz, Robert Perry, members of the Beyond Baroque Wednesday evening poetry workshop (in particular Ted Mico and Tom Laichas) and members of the Napa Valley Summer 2021 alumni cohort.

Special thanks to Jane Jacobson for observing "The great thing about a dream is that it doesn't create stuff which eventually needs to be taken to Goodwill."

COLOPHON

Cover and Interior Design
by Robert Perry
Dutch Poet Press and
Robert Perry Book Design
Palo Alto, California

Typeface for Display and Text
Seravek
designed by Eric Olson
Process Type Foundry
Minneapolis, Minnesota

Printed and distributed by
IngramSpark
La Vergne, Tennessee

www.ingramcontent.com/pod-product-compliance
Lightning Source LLC
Chambersburg PA
CBHW071918070526
44583CB00016B/2037